River Runners

The author and photographer would like to thank Waimarino Canoe Center and Bruce Webber Adventures for their help with this book.

CONTENTS

CHAPTER ONE

"Remember, Ben, lean back, hold the paddle high, and look straight ahead."

"OK," Ben quietly said, sounding more confident than he felt.

Water poured through the narrow outlet and flowed down the training slide.

Nervously, Ben edged the kayak to the top of the slide. Too afraid to look down, he glued his eyes to the line of the horizon. Far below him, the river ran past – ready to catch the kayak.

"Are you ready? 3... 2... 1... GO!" called the instructor.

The nose of the kayak tipped and, in one sweeping movement, slid forward.

Spray flew up, drenching Ben and blocking his view. Seconds later, the kayak flew off the end of the slide.

There was a loud *thwack* as the hull hit the water. Ben closed his eyes for the impact. He half expected to tip over. But the kayak remained upright and settled quietly on the water.

"Yahoo! Good for you. You did it!" called the group of spectators.

Then Ben heard the words he so desperately wanted to hear.

"That was really great, Ben. If you can master the training slide, you can handle anything," his instructor said.

For the rest of the afternoon, Ben watched the others try out the slide.

Toby, who was confident and thrived on a challenge, flew down the chute.

Next came Kara, her hair flying out behind her.

Then Sam shot down the slide, her face set in an excited grin.

Ben, smug with satisfaction, lay back on the long grass, watching the others.

He'd done it. No one could take that away from him.

It had been a week since Ben's parents had dropped him off at camp. He couldn't believe that at the beginning of the week he'd been afraid of even going out on the water!

He would be sad about having to go home tomorrow and leave his new friends and the river behind.

As the afternoon melted into evening, the children gathered around the campfire, talking and eating. Tonight was their last night. Tomorrow would be filled with sorting out gear, packing bags, and saying sad good-byes.

That night, Ben lay in his sleeping bag, wide awake, thinking about the past week.

Suddenly, he heard a sound.

"Psst, psst."

Ben sat up, instantly alert.

"Psst, Ben, are you awake?" Toby hissed. "I've got an idea. Let me in."

Toby crawled into the tent and sat down. "I've been thinking. How about we get up early tomorrow morning and do one last river run? A couple of hours is all we'll need. We can be back before the packing starts. What do you think?"

"I don't know, Toby. We're not supposed to go out in the kayaks without an instructor," Ben said.

"Oh, come on, Ben. We can do it. Look how well you managed the water slide today. It'll be great!"

A strange light flickered past the tent. Shadows appeared on the tent wall before subsiding again into darkness.

"What's that?" Toby whispcred.

The boys sat still, not daring to make a sound. The shadows hovered on the side of the tent.

Ben's heart felt as though it was going to burst out his throat. Beads of nervous sweat trickled down his neck.

A small spider scuttled its way down the tent walls and dropped onto Toby's face. He flung up his hand to flick it away. At the same time, he jabbed his elbow against the tent wall and into the shadow. Giggles broke out.

Poking their heads out of the tent, the two boys saw Sam and Kara. Their hands were tightly clamped across their mouths as they tried not to wake the rest of the camp with their laughter.

"What are you two doing?" Toby asked angrily.

"We know you're up to something. We want to be in on it," Kara demanded.

"Come on. Tell us," Sam begged.

"We're heading out in the morning for one final river run before we go," said Toby. "But you're not coming." He glanced at Ben. "They aren't, are they?"

Ben made his decision. "Yeah. It's one last river run. But it's just for Toby and me."

Sam and Kara looked at each other. They wouldn't be left out that easily. Sam began to think of a plan.

"You're not coming with us, so just beat it!" Toby hissed.

"Fine," said Sam. "Don't worry, we've got our own plans."

After the girls left, the two boys sat in the dark, whispering about the excitement of tomorrow's river run.

CHAPTER TWO

It seemed only seconds after he had fallen asleep that Ben's watch alarm went off. Quietly, he slipped out of his sleeping bag. He pulled on his wet suit, jacket, helmet, and life jacket and crept off to where the kayaks were kept.

Toby had already arrived and was dragging a blue kayak down to the entry point for the river run.

After choosing a kayak, Ben pulled a paddle from the pile and tried on a sprayskirt for size. This would protect him from the spray of water, which might otherwise fill the hull, making the kayak heavy and unmanageable.

It seemed as if a flock of butterflies were unleashed in Ben's stomach.

"OK. This is the plan." Ben couldn't detect any sign of nervousness in Toby's voice.

"We'll head downstream. Take your time through the Pencil Sharpener and around Potato Rock. Pull into the eddy just past the Pig Trough and we'll take a breather. I packed us some food and drinks, so we'll have breakfast there."

Ben could never get used to the unusual names given to the rocks and rapids on the river. Some names gave an idea of the conditions a kayaker could expect: the Roller Coaster, the Helicopter, and Pinball. Others were named after runs that hadn't gone as planned: the Pileup, Double Trouble, and Mother's Nightmare.

"OK," Ben replied, wondering if the whole thing was such a good idea. Still, Toby was a good kayaker; he knew what he was doing. If Toby could do it, then so could he. He remembered the quote from Franklin D. Roosevelt that his kayak instructor had told them: "The only thing we have to fear is fear itself..."

"Come on, let's go," said Toby.

Ben slid his legs into the nose of the kayak then stretched the neoprene sprayskirt around the lip of the cockpit. The kayak had now become an extension of his body.

Together, the boys slid into the river, its current easing them along gently. Small patterns swirled behind them as they dipped their paddles into the water.

CHAPTER THREE

"Sam, come on. The boys have gone," Kara whispered. "We need to be quick if we're going to follow them."

The girls dragged on their clothes, ran to the bike shed, and silently took out two of the bikes. They pushed them to the track by the riverbank.

Quickly, they hopped on the bikes and began peddling furiously, anxious to catch up with the two boys.

Ben cautiously paddled in Toby's wake. It took a few minutes, but soon Ben began to feel more confident. He slipped easily into a steady, rhythmic pattern. Just ahead, he could see the beginning of the white water.

Toby wove his way through the maze of rocks. Ben followed close behind.

As the river became quiet, they drew their kayaks alongside one another.

"Good for you," called Toby. "You're doing great. Do you think you're ready for the Pencil Sharpener?"

Ben knew the Pencil Sharpener well. He would never forget the white water that had tossed him in a wild, wet ride.

He would never forget the way it had spit him out through a narrow chute, leaving him drenched and exhilarated.

Ben could hear the roar of the Pencil Sharpener long before he could see it. The river began to narrow, and curls of white water shaved the side of the cliffs, pounding their tiny crafts as they flew down the course.

From the bushes, the girls caught fleeting glimpses of the boys' exciting ride. They were envious but also a little nervous for them.

Surging through a big dip between two tall rocks, the boys passed the Pig Trough and quickly entered a calm eddy. Turning their kayaks toward a sheltered bay, the boys paddled in to rest for a while.

A mixture of spray and perspiration trickled together and ran in tiny rivulets down their faces. The boys laughed. They had made it!

Suddenly, a loud scream echoed from across the river. "Aaaaahhh!" Sam's bike came crashing through the bushes. The bike came to a sudden stop, throwing Sam over the handlebars and into the river.

"What was that noise?" the boys both exclaimed.

Kara emerged from the bushes and helped a laughing Sam out of the water and back onto the bank.

"What are you two doing here?" Ben asked in surprise.

"Well, you two seemed determined not to let us go kayaking with you," retorted Sam. "So we decided to go on our own adventure!"

"Well, since you're here, you might as well have something to eat with us," Toby said, smiling.

After breakfast, Ben said, "You two stick to peddling, and we'll stick to paddling. We'll see you at Red Knight Corner."

The boys eased the kayaks into the water, and with a splash, they nosed them out into the current.

CHAPTER FOUR

By now, the sun had fully risen from behind the hills and was lifting the dew from the grass, sending tendrils of steam into the air.

The Tsunami, the last set of rapids before the end of the run, was drawing close. Ben felt a flood of fear.

"I can't do it, Toby. I know I can't," Ben called out across the roar of angry water.

"You can. You have to," Toby shouted back. "There's nowhere else to go!" And, with his paddle held high above his head in a gesture of defiance, Toby disappeared into the frothing, gurgling mass of water.

The din of the pounding water drowned any last words Toby may have tried to add. Within moments, Ben, too, was caught in the grip of the river. He dipped his paddle furiously from side to side, sometimes using it as a rudder to swerve past protruding rocks. His eyes were wide with fear. Time and time again, he waited for the sickening crunch of his kayak hitting a rock.

It seemed an eternity before he finally emerged from the Tsunami.

From their vantage point beside the river, the two girls watched the boys approach the rapids. A horrified look appeared on Sam's face. "Oh, Kara! Look!" she cried.

At the tip of the rapids, where the currents converged, the white water picked up Toby's kayak and tossed it through the air like a matchstick. Struggling to stay upright, Toby caught his paddle against the side of a rock, upsetting his balance. The kayak flew through the rapids, emerging from the other side, overturned.

CHAPTER FIVE

The girls raced along the edge of the river, hoping the current would drift the kayak within their grasp.

Ben paddled over to Toby's kayak as fast as he could, using the nose of his craft to push it toward the river's edge.

Kara rushed into the water. "Help me drag it in, Sam!" she called.

Together, they dragged the kayak into shallow water and quickly flipped it upright. It was empty, and there was no sign of Toby.

"Look for him, Ben! Look for him!" Sam shouted as she ran along the riverbank.

Ben turned his kayak back into the current and began paddling as fast as he could. He knew time was short. If Toby had been carried away, he'd be heading straight for Devil's Elbow. He would never survive the twenty-one-foot fall.

"Sam, get help," Kara shouted as she rushed along the river's edge, searching for the purple-and-yellow life jacket. As she pushed through the bushes, a scrap of purple cloth caught her attention.

"Ben! Ben!" she screamed. "I can see something. Help me. Quick!"

Ben turned his kayak around and furiously paddled toward the bank. As he navigated his way through the rocks, he saw Toby caught in a tangle of branches. Ben pulled off his helmet and swam through the rapids to where Toby lay near the riverbank.

Gently, Ben pushed Toby up out of the water so Kara could grasp his life jacket. As the wet and exhausted Toby was pulled up onto the bank, his eyes flickered, and he smiled weakly.

"I did it, Kara. Boy, did I do it!" he murmured.

As Ben and Kara were making Toby as comfortable as possible, they heard Sam and one of the camp leaders talking and rushing toward them.

Toby looked at Ben. "How are we going to explain our way out of this one?" he mumbled.

"Don't worry, Toby," Ben said, smiling. "I'll tell the whole story, one rapid at a time!"

AUTHOR AND PHOTOGRAPHER

Andy and I enjoy the outdoors and love to participate in as many different adventure sports as possible. Scuba diving, skydiving, caving, kayaking; you name it, we've done it. The more exciting it is, the more we enjoy it.

Eventually, Andy started photographing adventure sports.